Embers Of The Soul

When the lines of the inanimate world blur

Shrija Singh

BookLeaf Publishing

India | USA | UK

Made with ❤ on the BookLeaf Publishing Platform

www.bookleafpub.in

www.bookleafpub.com

Dedication

To Maa — for letting me be the winner.
To Yashu — for being my honest mirror.
To Papa — for letting me step into the sea,
letting me risk and be guilt-free.
To Kishan — for this wonderful start.
To Rewa — for inspiring the love of this art.

Preface

This collection comes straight from the heart, and it finds its final resting place there as well. The poems reflect the stories and themes we experience every day.

Increasingly, the use of personification has been highlighted in these pieces – thereby blurring the lines of the inanimate world.

They delve into our fears—sometimes perceived as unrealistic, yet at other times, deeply overwhelming. The verses serve as a reminder of time's power, personifying how the inanimate world knows us and those who wear masks for the world around them.

The collection also touches on the little frustrations of daily life: from the beeping messages in extended family groups, to the seemingly trivial moments like the boiling of milk, which—if not watched—can transform a warm, sunny evening into an unexpected task of mopping. It also addresses the universal struggle of losing things right when they're needed.

Love, heartbreak, betrayal, and the painful yet necessary process of letting go also take center stage. There are tributes to our unsung heroes— the silent helpers whom we often forget until their services are no longer needed.

The poems capture the simplicity and wonder of shopping with parents, the joy of family gatherings, and the innocence of a child's perspective.

A great deal of self-reflection on the past, present, and future gave birth to this work.

It is an ode to the experiences of the soul on life's journey—sometimes fading, and at other times, glistening brightly.

And so, I present to you *Embers of the Soul.*

Acknowledgements

To my mother, the light who kept me steady when the path felt uncertain, and the careful hand that edited every stumble – thank you for everything.

To my brother, Shreyash, who lent his creative eye to the cover – thank you for helping me make a first impression of this work I could be proud of.

To my father, who taught me the art of balancing dreams with reality – your faith in me allowed this one to come true.

To Rewa Ravind, whose early encouragement gave my words the wings they needed to soar.

To Kishan, the tireless supporter who celebrated every milestone like it was his own – I could not have asked for a better motivator.

To Book Leaf Publishing — thank you for giving me a chance I found by serendipity, and for believing in my little universe of words.

And to every kind soul who urged me to share these poems with the world — this is as much yours as it is mine.

Finally, to you, dear reader:
Thank you for opening these pages.
Thank you for making this dream real.

1. The Room's Warm Gravity

In my dreamworld across the cove,
Lemongrass tea on the stove,
The air thick with the scent of baked flour,
On the floor, tiled in print of the daisy flower,
Scattered crumbs from cinnamon delights,
Evidence of indulgent nights,
Nibbled onto by the little ball of fluff,
Who acts as if he is the owner — so tough.

Dodging the items with mouth full of stolen rewards,
Dashing across the hall towards
A wall lined with books,
Opposite flowerpots adorned with witty looks,
Each telling a story —
he bliss of the pictorial allegory!
Each with a personality —
Oh, the room's warm gravity!

From the outside world's burdens,

Shielded by rust-hued, timeworn curtains,
So tall and so warm,
Adding to the room's hidden charm.
Sunlight coming in from the stained glass,
Casting a glow on statues of golden brass.

Ancestors' pictures on the wall,
Kind eyes of wisdom on the room they fall —
A beautiful reverie to behold
In the world so cold.

In this cozy, cherished, dreamlike fold,
This happiness — no store could hold.
Warm springs of pure solitude
Wash away the heavy stains of sorrow, leaving only
gratitude.

2. Growing up is a Scam

In the horse stand,
Of the wonderland.
Is the pony, a pure bliss,
It departs on its adventure after its mother's kiss.

A baby by age,
Roaming outside its wooden cage.
Its leather-black fur,
Creating amongst the onlookers a stir.

Glistening in the February sun,
It gallops and sometimes likes to run.
Where Greenfield and uneven pathways,
Are preferred by it over the city's reckless highways.

Carefree it goes around.
Doesn't turn at every sound.
The pure joy it has found.
By reckless customs it isn't bound.

Oh, dear pony please stay the same!
Growing up, a foolish aim.
It does not bring the glory or fame.
Leaving this persona? Oh, that would be a shame!

If the grown-up experience should be given a rate,
It barely makes a weak eight!
Don't fall for the bait,
Unless that way forges your fate!

3. The Sea's Greeting

Splashes hit my feet —
Oh, the cool water feels great!
I forget all my past defeat.

Am I really scared of the sea?
Or does the fear linger,
Just within the perceived image of what should be me?
In the water dives my finger —
Oh, the cool water feels great.
Deceit is the sea's subtle trait,
And suddenly, I remember the sea's previous ire;
Playing with it is putting bare hands on fire.

But the water feels great.
Don't forget the sea's innate.
For some, its experiences hold thrill;
To some, it is the uncle who is super chill;
To others, it offers lavish meals of krill;
Some, it does kill.

In the Ocean of possibility,
I choose life.
With great responsibility,
I take away the sea's knife.

4. The Family Group Parody

Strings of messages beep all day,
Separated by distance, but somehow still find a way.

The older ones and their timeless gnaw,
While the younger ones just sit and yawn.

Wishing one spouse on their anniversary,
The other missed by the sharp memory.

Celebrating achievements small or big,
Wise old souls enjoying their favourite gig.

"Good morning" messages with beautiful flowers so
bright,
Forwarded messages arrive in showers, day, and night.

No celebration ever misses their eyes,
Congratulatory messages full of sweet lies.

Floods of social media links drown the group,

Often, we see dances of their favourite troupe.

A group that you neither join by will,
Yet leaving? Oh, you wouldn't dare still.

They teach us that sometimes distance seems necessary,
Fake love is an unworn neglected accessory.

5. Melted Honey Hazel Hues

The honey wants to drip,
But, held so tight by your eyes' grip.
Oh, the honey glistens in the sun!
May I dip in it my stale bun?

Soft, warm colour,
A perfect day in summer.
Your eyes are a universe of their own-
My mind is completely blown.

Your eyes are like a beautiful moon,
Can I lose myself in them soon?
A blink reveals the curled eyelash.
In a beauty contest - your eyes would win the sash.

The mole on both sides, at the perfect distance,
So carefully placed, I can't miss its presence.
If I were to love a part of you forever,
It would be certainly your eyes - so clever.

In a world filled with colourful eyes,
I believe the melted honey hazel hue never lies!

6. The Mask of Façade

The honey wants to drip,
But, held so tight by your eyes' grip.
Oh, the honey glistens in the sun!
May I dip in it my stale bun?

Soft, warm colour,
A perfect day in summer.
Your eyes are a universe of their own-
My mind is completely blown.

Your eyes are like a beautiful moon,
Can I lose myself in them soon?
A blink reveals the curled eyelash.
In a beauty contest - your eyes would win the sash.

The mole on both sides, at the perfect distance,
So carefully placed, I can't miss its presence.
If I were to love a part of you forever,
It would be certainly your eyes - so clever.

In a world filled with colourful eyes,
I believe the melted honey hazel hue never lies!

7. Into the unknown, letting the Past Go

Onto the new beginnings, I depart,
From old stories, I grow apart.

The soulful hymn of belonging
Would turn into reunion's longing.

The time moves fast;
We shed skins of the past.

Within the seat of new fears,
Last time we shed old tears.

Old seniors would turn into mentors;
I would face new dementors.

Juniors would be replacing my position —
But will the heart also have a deposition?

Kindness and chatter

Replaced by firmness, lost playful banter.

My heart will always pour out the reason:
The transition from one to the next —
The transition is from connecting in person
To connecting over text.

8. Trust is a Boat you Sail on Once

Pouring coffee of the kettle,
As he sat on his seat,
Uncomfortably shifting he decided to settle,
Tarnished by his past defeat,
Seems to have changed his heart of metal.
Betrayal of past, will he again cheat?

He opened his mouth for a while,
She opened her whole existence to him.
He listened to her, he gave her a hope of a beautiful
senile,
The gushing feeling, like downing a bottle of gin,
The care, the understanding, the respect she saw from a
mile.
The comforting giggles and mischievous grin,
All were bonuses in the pile,
But, in her mind the past betrayal still would prickle and
pin.

Again, he got her addicted,
And left her to deal with her own monsters.
Wasn't this betrayal predicted?
He was for sure a hooded impostor,
She was forewarned but trusted what was depicted-
If she heard the advice of her mother-
Even in her mind the thoughts always conflicted-
Had she listened she would not have to bother.
Decrypting his texts for meaning that was earlier
encrypted,
To witness hope's quiet murder.

The void was always before,
The void was left, therefore.
But the hope that answered the help's cry,
Now, simply doesn't want to try.

His smile again resembled the grinch's grin,
Trusting him, obviously another sin.
Bitter coffee made of the rusted gin.
Hope lies on line so thin.
To leave you to sink, he has cut off your fin.
The monster of him in his cold, dull silver skin,
Betrayal made hope wail, locked back in a deep cabin.

9. The torch of thee, the Dimness of me

Where others find eerie,
Started a love story so merry-
But, ended so teary,
The tears filled the Ocean in my theory.

She saw straight into my heart.
Oh, we could never be apart!
Her eyes a pure work of art.
"Till death do us part!"

Sunshine doesn't reach us,
Travellers of shallow waters often fuss.
The description fits, just as I must.
In her I find the soul's food, my yellow chamaecytisus.

To become truly one,
We still have a long journey to run.
Onze reis shall be fun,
But will she still continue to shine like sun?

Or the dreary night of me,
Dim the torch of thee,
Should I warn her to flee?
Before she becomes permanent in my reverie.

In the water she is the fire,
All my heart's desire.
But as we become one, it will be our pyre.
Why is our situation so dire?

As we love thyself,
We shall lose ourself.
But the loss that I fear is not of myself,
Rather the loss of herself.

Don't want to dim or take away her light.
That fear will always bite.
I will leave her despite,
Just to be morally right.

10. Echoes from the Toy Box

When I first met you at the age of three;
Your eyes lit up at the sight of me,
The glee in your little voice squeaked – "whee!"
We played together, wild and free.

When I was the town's new talk,
Familiar older toys faded, left in disinterest's lock.
Piece by piece you built me every day,
A complete picture of the barn of hay.

Then I met your best friend,
Solving puzzles became the new trend.
I was hard, a puzzling feat,
Yet you dove in, never admitting defeat.

And then, the dreaded day came when I was not difficult
How much longer could I be your heart's catapult?
I stopped boggling you at eight,
To play with a 3+ puzzle it was too late.

The newness of me had faded,
My fate completely jaded.
Bent corners of the cardboard within me,
Were hidden to protect your honour, I see!

I was no more the favourite star,
Picked up only when new toys left you bored afar.
Lost piece by piece and shred by shred,
My charm dimmed with each tear I shed.

I am the forgotten puzzle of your old toy box,
Once tucked in your Christmas sock.

11. Heartfelt Echoes in Glass

Your morning eyes,
Blinking dreamily in the rays of unwelcome lights.
A pretty face scared with sleep marks,
Of your lucky pillow.
Glistening in the light,
Are the bodies of the dead soldiers -
Of your eyes last night's battles lost.
Toothbrush in your uneven teeth,
Shielded by a smile so pretty.
Can I get over it honestly?
I reflect you faithfully!
Can you see my heart in it?

You moved out of my frame,
And I had a dull wall to reflect on.

You stop by again, bringing bright colours of day to me.
Your afternoon eyes,
Happy for the contended meal that you just ate.
You pick your teeth, looking at me.

You pout at your belly, glancing at me -
You say you ate too much -
You say you look so fat!
Oh, sweetheart you are perfect.
Faded pink lipstick on your lips,
Dreamy girl vibes you give.
Can I get over it honestly?
I reflect you faithfully!
Can you see my truth in it?

You moved out of my frame,
And I am left with the boring wall.

You stop by as the sun dips, cloaked in evening's
embrace.
Your evening eyes,
I could stare at them for a while.
You have make-up on -
Smoky eyes hiding the true dream-
Red lipstick on your fuller lips.
I think you are ready for a date.
Is it to find a mate?
You look so surreal!
Can I get over it honestly?
I reflect you faithfully!
Can you see my desire in it?

You step away from my frame,
And I'm left with emptiness, a silent wall.

You stop by in the dark hours of doom.
Your night eyes,
Tarnished by a smudged mascara.
Another failed attempt at love!
Wasn't he meant to smudge the lipsticks?
You look into me.
No smile I see.
You brush your teeth.
You look weary.
But you are always beautiful.
Sweetheart, give me a chance to love?
Can I get over it honestly?
I reflect you faithfully!
Can you see my soul in it?

You moved out of my frame,
And I reflect an empty wall with a broken heart.

(I wish I could speak, not just reflect,
But all I do is mirror your pain,
Waiting for you to see the truth I hold.
I wish you could see what I reflect,
Not just the stillness of my silence.

I wonder how long I can endure,
A prisoner to silence, my love never returned.)

12. The Kingdom of Clutter

The perfect purple frock,
Guarded by the big mess's lock,
The search, a drill full of mock,
What I need appears to be out of stock!

But this princess knows the kingdom's reality,
The reminiscent dress popping up with all sincerity,
Visibility impaired by the mess's grandiosity,
All tossed together in the mess's majority.

I know the queen who can help me navigate,
But I am dodging the scolding fate,
The problem, therefore, I am not stating straight,
Even though I would be late.

The clock ticks by,
Punctuality of soul makes frantic cry,
All I am doing to my soul is tell a lie,
I accept my sad fate with a sigh.

I call for my mother urgently,
She appears emergently,
I ask for her help immediately,
She looks at the mess gently.

She finds my dress triumphantly,
The mockery's grin spreads instantly,
I get reprimanded for the mess amazingly,
Betrayal of the frock affected my life brilliantly.

13. The Sweet Hoax

As I guide my little daughter of three,
Checking the shopping list on hand.
Slight tilt on my right knee,
As her little soft fingers wrap around my hand.
Eyes glisten up as we enter for her shopping spree,
The arcade - her wonderland.

Empty cart she runs and tries to grab,
Her tiny arms, too small to pull it though.
She grips her chosen cart as tight as a crab.
"Daddy, why do they put all the carts in a row?"
While I pull out the cart, she studies the arcade's map,
I say determined, "Sweety, let us go."

The cart fills up with diapers, wipes, and towels
for her little sister
"What for me daddy?"
She asks me wearing a look so sinister
"We will get you your favorite candy."
"Is that all we are going to get mister?"

With a mischievous smile I say "Also my favorite
brandy."

As grocery shopping gets over,
She runs to the aisle of toys.
Filled with dolls and sometimes their irritating lover,
At this stage she likes toys of both girls and boys.
She placed the butterfly wings in cart, over the leaves of
clover
I look at her with a frown and mouth "That is not the
best choice."
She puts on her most innocent face,
Me being fully aware, the cuteness is a complete
faux.
She tugs at her frill frock delicate white lace,
Eyes summoned the crocodile tears, a complete
coax.
The art of deception, she which she will soon ace,
Learning from her mother, the sweet hoax.

And yet I would fall,
Knowing well the cuteness is a complete faux.
A man six feet tall,
Yet fooled by a coax.
Losing to a tantrum of this missy in middle of a mall,
Unable to get past the sweet hoax.

I lift her carrying her on my shoulder,
While she kicks her little feet, screaming loud.
I am a man looking like a heartless boulder,
Heart breaking inside, as she smacks her lips in a pout.

At a safe distance from the wretched toy aisle,
I finally place her down.
She won the match in pure style,
I am now the ultimate clown.
She runs far away, looks somewhat like a mile,
She turns back, and gives me a frown.

The beeps of the billing counter,
Drown the memory of my past defeat.
While I feel a tug at my knee, I flounder,
The malicious winner was again near my feet.
Although, she won at the last encounter,
All she did was cheat.

I load the purchased goods into my cart,
While I see her hands neatly in the back.
I raise my eyebrows unskilled at this art,
Fearing she had stolen an item off the rack.
Then a sudden knot grew in my heart,
How in parenthood could I slack?

I asked her to show me her hands,

She produced a red lipstick immediately.
"I took this from my make-up stands."
She mouths kindly.

"Everyone got gifts for the baby, people from highlands
Coastlands, farmlands, or homelands.
Ladies flocked around sissy from parklands
Or Aunts from pinelands."

"Mommy likes red,
This one is for mommy.
This would look nice on her beautiful head,
She sometimes feels alone in the lobby."

I realised, although, I must reprimand her for
stealing,
All the love wanted to do was healing.

Heart in dismay, I knelt to my equal's level,
'Sweetheart, that's lovely—but we have to pay for stuff.'
She nodded, and I wondered to me, this devil,
She is indeed like her mother, so tough.

14. The Mischief of Milk

The serene creamy elixir of life,
Holding sometimes a sweet strife.

Mix it with care,
And joy fills the air.

Present in almost everything good,
Increases the taste of food.

But funny is its boiling game,
Almost as famous as its own fame.

Watch it for hours,
Patience could fill in jars.

Turn away once,
And behold the dunce.

The anger of it creates unwelcome showers,
Mopping the spilled mess for hours.

The air now reeks with milky stench,
Our noses scrunch, our fingers clench.

A healthy option it still is -
Truly nature's creamy bliss.

15. The Power of Time

Time is the king,
Time makes the slave.
Time so indecisive,
Goes in a way that never let's you be brave.

Fast is the lullaby,
Fast is the life,
When you enjoy the thing-
Just like the ravishes of Henry the VIII's wife.

Slow is the rhythm,
Slow is your life,
Whenever you loathe the thing,
Whenever your moment is strife.

16. A Threat to Their Normal

In a world of black and white;
I was the yellow.
Where people led a life being right;
I led a life mellow.

While others reeked sanity,
My redolence was considered derangement.
They look down on my supposed profanity,
Thereby making me suffer from estrangement.

Deep down they know I am a threat,
To social norms, which are boring and irrelevant.
The thought of transformation is what makes them
upset,
Change for the better was never their element.

17. Our Boats, Apart

And then we stopped talking,
Completely unsure of what went lacking.
While efforts from neither were slacking,
In silence, our life was chalking.

Uneasy stiffness of silence prevailed.
The soul's sadness was fully jailed.
In two different boats, our journey sailed—
All our shared plans had failed.

A void of silent storm,
This was my heart's home.
With fate carved into stone,
Could I borrow some time, maybe as a loan?

Beautiful moonlight, once bathing us, now haunts.
The twinkling stars above feel like cruel taunts.
How can I forget what this soul still wants?
Moving ahead is a task that daunts.

18. Relatives and Revelries

Each house-proud spouse, scrubbing with care,
Prepping the home for guests to share.

Welcoming kin from every relation,
Beds arranged in tight formation.

The relatives arriving from near and far,
Off to the station goes the pickup car.

Loading people beyond its actual capacity,
We drive home with sheer audacity.

Pickles, sweet and sour, fill the jar,
Open bags – behold the bazaar.

Bringing lots of love and joy,
Kids rejoice in each brand-new toy.

Moments we treasure,
Memories we'll keep forever.

19. Things That Knew Me

If the tree that grew beside my childhood home could
narrate my younger giggle,
It'd hum the tune of tiny toes and memories that
wriggle.
The little forgotten dime in my pocket would sometimes
jiggle,
Jumping around often I would wiggle.

If the familiar old garden could narrate the tale of my
lover,
Secluded hidden bushes hid us under its cover,
Moving through shadows, it would gently manoeuvre,
With eyes our love would devour.

If moon revealed our quite conversations,
Often venting in anger's slow sedation,
Letting out my simmering frustration,
Oh—my secrets would spill in such personification!

If the ocean could portray my salty tale,

It could tell all the times I had grown pale,
As my journey became increasingly stale,
All the instances that made me frail.

But the blowing wind often describes me,
It still refers to me as a good flea,
A careless bee on petals free,
But tethered deep, unknowingly.

20. Breaking the Chain

All my stress,
Has created such a mess,
So many days haven't reduced it any less.

Such a fuss,
I just want to cuss,
A pain of the mess's pus.

Oh, I wish I was hit by a lovely breeze of pure calm,
Take me out of this state of pure alarm,
Like the peace of working is my house's farm.

I wish I could do away with my unfortunate pain,
In my life it has caused such a strain,
I wish I could somehow break this chain.

21. To the Bravest Soul I Know

Hi my dearest,
You are now my nearest.

You were so fearless,
Full of happiness, life tearless.

In the room, you were so loud,
And in all honesty, I am so proud.

You have done things right,
All decisions were taken without any fright.

Growing up with knees that often scrapped,
Even surpassing the broken heart that once ached.

All my fears you have faced,
In our sweet life you have aced.

I am proud of the one girl you are,

I hope your feelings for this lady is not far?

Thank you for dreaming,
With happiness I am beaming.